BREATHTAKING NEW means of communicating and creating; of accessing, storing, and organizing massive amounts of information; of buying and selling everything from financial advice to the latest Los Angeles Philharmonic recording to a chauffeured drive across the city – the Internet has brought all these things and much, much more. A platform of ceaseless innovation, it has transformed our lives, mostly for the better, in a remarkably short time.

And America has led the revolution. The Internet's dazzling technologies and infrastructure, drawing in billions and billions of dollars in yearly investment, remain disproportionately American. Web-based U.S. firms like Amazon, Facebook, and Google span the globe as immediately recognizable brands. Ten of the world's 15 largest websites are American. For technology visionary George Gilder, the Internet is "at the heart of America's world leadership" and is "America's gift to the world."

All that is now under threat. In late February 2015, after an unprecedented intervention in its affairs by President Barack Obama, a purportedly independent Federal Communications Commission (FCC) voted along party lines (three Democrats yea, two Republicans nay) to impose extensive regulatory controls on this vibrant, expanding digital universe. The main goal of the "Obamanet," as the *Wall Street Journal* christened the new regulatory regime, is to mandate "network neutrality," a technical term that, activists say, simply means requiring Internet service providers (ISPs), such as Time Warner and Verizon, to treat all the data surging through their systems in the same way.

That may sound benign, but the more you examine the technical and regulatory stakes, the more you realize that the FCC's power grab is a very bad thing. Should the Obamanet take root, unending litigation and uncertainty will result, dampening investment and stifling enterprise in the most dynamic sector of the U.S economy. Established Internet firms increasingly will try to win exemptions from the rules, creating a system of preferment that would have horrified the Founding Fathers. More troubling still is that the Obamanet could bring new efforts to restrict political speech – an end long sought by many on the left.

The Road to Internet Serfdom

What encouraged the Internet's efflorescence of creativity was an early bipartisan consensus among American leaders that the Internet should largely be free from regulation – "permissionless," as Adam Thierer, a scholar at the Mercatus Center, puts it. That is, anyone – you, me, Mark Zuckerberg, Martha Stewart, the local hardware store – could use the Internet to start a website, launch an app, or experiment with business models without first getting the government's OK. "The Internet wouldn't be a heavily regulated utility like the old phone system," explains L. Gordon Crovitz in the *Wall Street Journal*. Instead, it would be an "information service," which the

The more you examine the technical and regulatory stakes, the more you realize that the FCC's power grab is a very bad thing.

government would mostly leave alone. The language of the Telecommunications Act of 1996 reflected this market-friendly vision: the policy of the United States would preserve "the vibrant and competitive free market that presently exists for the Internet ... unfettered by Federal or State regulation."

The leave-it-alone consensus held for roughly a decade – from the mid-1990s, when the Clinton administration first opened the Internet for commerce, until the mid-2000s. What ended it was the rise of a movement of left-wing "netroots" activists, politicians, and lobbying groups. Funded heavily by financier

George Soros, the movement sought to get the government to impose network neutrality – a phrase coined by Columbia law professor Tim Wu in 2003 – on ISPs.

Those companies wanted to manage their broadband "pipes" more actively – and more profitably – offering, say, superfast express lanes for content providers and consumers willing to pay more, or balancing traffic loads to make service smoother for all users, casual email sender and bandwidth glutton alike. The advocates and their allies viewed such practices darkly. If the ISPs got their way, the argument went, they would lord it over their service areas, give preferential treatment to well-heeled allied sites, and even slow down or block the content of rivals and small start-ups. The "broadband barons" would make themselves the gatekeepers of the Internet, shaking down everyone for more and more money in exchange for less and less service. The open Internet would be dead. An Internet of enclosures and walls would arise in its place. Innovation would suffer.

On behalf of the people, therefore, the government had to intervene and guarantee that all data received equal treatment. No "digital discrimination" by ISPs should be allowed, ever. The ISPs had to be forced to stay neutral and their conduits kept "dumb," with all the intelligence in the system located in the senders and receivers using the Internet. Harvard law professor Lawrence Lessig described the ideal in his book *Code and Other Laws of Cyberspace*: "Like a daydreaming postal worker, the network simply moves the data and leaves its interpretation to the applications at either end."

A first push to get the FCC to mandate network neutrality came in 2007. Two years earlier, the agency had issued a "policy statement" – not an official regulation but four suggested norms – to guide the future of the Internet. Users, the principles ran, should be able to: 1) access the lawful content of their choice; 2) run the applications and services of their choice, "subject to the needs of law enforcement"; 3) connect legal devices of their choice, as long as they didn't harm the network; and 4) benefit from competition among ISPs and other Internet firms. Together with other activists, a nonprofit inaptly called Free Press petitioned the commission to enforce the policy statement against the cable giant Comcast, which was slowing down the bandwidth-hogging BitTorrent file sharing among some of its network users so that other users' service didn't degrade. Comcast soon reached a private agreement with BitTorrent to ease congestion and improve service for everyone. The FCC nevertheless proceeded to censure Comcast for violating the ideal of an open Internet and demanded greater disclosure of its network-management practices. Comcast sued, and in 2010 the Court of Appeals for the D.C. Circuit ruled that the commission lacked the statutory authority to tell the cable company what to do.

The Obama-era FCC issued an "Open Internet Order" in 2010 that again called for network neutrality, but in January 2014 it also lost at the D.C. Circuit for exceeding its regulatory power. FCC Chairman Thomas Wheeler, a Democrat appointed by Obama, then began work on a "third way" that would permit ISPs considerable freedom to deploy smart network-management practices while still banning website throttling, blocking of legal content, and other anticompetitive practices. Wheeler believed that the D.C. Circuit's decision left open a path to such a compromise.

That's when the Obama administration got more directly involved – going so far, the *Wall Street Journal* later reported in a front-page exclusive, as to set up a secretive "parallel version" of the FCC within the White House. The shadow commission began meeting with media activists and representatives of various Internet companies, including Tumblr and Kickstarter, to devise a more comprehensive version of network neutrality and make it stick the third time around. They settled on was what some called the nuclear option: getting the FCC to reclassify the Internet as a "common carrier" public utility under Title II of the Communications Act of 1934, a regulatory framework designed for the monopolistic phone service of that era. That reclassification would give the commission vast new authority to regulate "unjust or unreasonable discrimination in charges, practices, classifications, regulations, facilities, or services" across the Internet. Regulators would be able to dictate neutrality – and much more – with such power.

One of the leading activists, Marvin Ammori, a consultant for tech firms, began campaigning for wider public support for the idea. He spoke in May 2014 with staff from HBO's comedy news program *Last Week Tonight With John Oliver*, and a few weeks later, the show's host aired a long rant urging web "trolls" to bombard the FCC with emails demanding neutrality. "We need you to get out there, and for once in your lives, focus your indiscriminate rage in a useful manner," Oliver thundered. A tidal wave of pro-neutrality comments overwhelmed the FCC's comment system.

Nov. 10 proved a turning point. "The day began with Mr. Obama issuing a surprise video insisting on the most extreme regulation for the Internet, submitting it to laws written in the 1930s for Ma Bell," recounts Crovitz, whose writing on technology issues has been exemplary. "The same morning, a group of protesters swarmed Mr. Wheeler's house, blocked access to his car, and demanded that he obey the president." A shaken Wheeler viewed the video and protests as coordinated, as internal

---

The Obama administration set up a secretive "parallel version" of the FCC within the White House. The shadow commission began meeting with media activists and representatives of various Internet companies.

---

emails subsequently examined by Congress showed. But he soon surrendered to the Saul Alinsky–style intimidation. Several months later, over the outraged protests of the FCC's two Republican commissioners, the Obamanet was born, a dense 300-plus-page order (eight pages of rules, the rest footnotes trying to explain them) making its arrival official.

As one of the dissident commissioners observed, the pressure from the White House was shocking. "I've served under a number of different chairmen during administrations of Republican and Democratic affiliation," antitrust expert Ajit Pai told *Reason*'s Nick Gillespie. "I've never seen anything as high profile as this. … Creating a YouTube video and [posting to the White House's website] very specific prescriptions as to what this agency should do, followed by the agency suddenly changing course from where it was to mimic the president's plan, I think suggests that the independence of the agency has been compromised to some extent."

* * *

The first thing to say about the FCC's Title II move is that even on its own terms, it's unwarranted. In issuing its 2010 Open Internet Order, the commission could point to just four actions in the Internet's history that neutrality rules might have prevented. "Even these four are questionable," note Geoffrey A. Manne and R. Ben Sperry of the International Center for Law and Economics, "and all of them were resolved without the heavy hand of net neutrality." The Obamanet order, too, offers no evidence of systematic harm to consumers to justify the FCC's sweeping takeover. Indeed, ISPs have yet to offer fast and slow lanes to the public for different prices, and they haven't been throttling or blocking sites. Writes lawyer Michael Rosen for the website the American: "Imposing the heavy-handed remedy of Title II regulation resembles nothing so much as blasting an ant-hill with a bazooka." Pai agrees: "The most important thing that people need to know is that this is a solution that won't work to a problem that simply doesn't exist." To understand why the Internet has remained open, look no further than the free market: If you're an ISP and you're trying to attract customers, why would you block content that they might want?

Ah, some network-neutrality supporters respond, that market incentive might work if ISPs had to fight for customers, but many Americans lack a choice of Internet providers. Without the FCC's protections, these consumers would have to accept what their monopolistic provider force-fed them or go without Internet access. But that contention, which had some plausibility a decade ago, is less accurate every day. Spurred by competition and the prospect of greater profits, ISPs have spent hugely in recent years – more than $180 billion in 2011 and 2012 alone – to improve and expand broadband service, and consumers have benefited. Seven out of 10 Americans can now choose between at least two fixed broadband connections of 10 megabits per second or higher, the U.S. Department of

Commerce reports; other estimates are even higher. Add 3G and LTE wireless service, which blanket the country, and you've got lots more choice. (Such choice isn't limited to the well-off, by the way: lower-income groups have been boosting their use of smartphones more than any other group.) If you don't like your ISP – and some have drawn legitimate fire for abysmal consumer service – you've increasingly got options.

Further, what ISPs offer in the United States has been getting better and better. Broadband speed accelerated 21 percent in 2014, according to the *State of the Internet Report*, published by the tech company Akamai. Nine of the 15 fastest broadband locations in the world are now in the U.S. Costs continue to fall: the price of moving data across the Internet has plummeted 30 percent a year in the new millennium. Internet traffic – measured either per resident or per user – is higher in the U.S. than in any other country except South Korea, technology researcher Bret Swanson found in a survey for the American Enterprise Institute; in fact, per-user traffic here is twice that of tech-obsessed Japan. "If you look at the Akamai *State of the Internet Report*... or other objective data," Pai observes, "there's no question that America is better off, especially considering our relatively lower population density, in terms of deployment, speeds, prices, whatever metric you choose." Writes Wi-Fi co-inventor Richard Bennett, with understatement: "The Internet is working well, so it's not obvious that the FCC needs to help it."

And would it be so awful if ISPs did charge customers more for lightning-fast lanes for heavy-bandwidth products – or for other innovations that treated data unequally? Consumers happily pay more to have FedEx overnight an important package. How would it be any different to pay more for, say, super-fast movie streaming? Or for a security-enhanced network? Or for 3-D holograms? As long as service for basic users isn't degraded, who loses out with such product differentiation? Perhaps some consumers would like an inexpensive phone that provides a "discriminatory" package of basic service and a special fast stream of HBO Go, letting people watch the network remotely but not counting against their data plans. Should the FCC prevent such choices, as Dutch regulatory authorities recently did, on network-neutrality grounds? And what is so unjust about requiring massive content providers like Netflix and YouTube – together consuming *half* of Internet bandwidth in the U.S. and Canada during peak periods – to pay extra to help ease network congestion? Joshua Wright of the Federal Trade Commission (FTC), arguing against the FCC's Internet takeover before the House Judiciary Committee, points to extensive empirical economic research – ignored by the FCC's order – showing that these kinds of arrangements that are banned by network neutrality "very rarely result in consumer harm." They "often provide substantial benefits for consumers," he added, including increased output, higher quality, and lower overall prices. These arrangements are a normal part of a functioning market economy.

Indeed, network neutrality is at odds with

In issuing its 2010 Open Internet Order, the FCC could point to just four actions in the Internet's history that neutrality rules might have prevented.

---

many of the now standard practices that have helped make today's Internet the market cornucopia that it is, as University of Pennsylvania technology scholar Christopher Yoo shows in his informative 2013 book *The Dynamic Internet.* The Internet has evolved, diversified, and put heavy new demands on networks – such as those made by social media, tablets, and Netflix streaming videos, to name just a few innovations that have become mainstream in the past several years. During this time, ISPs and other Internet firms had engaged in all sorts of discriminatory engineering to manage the data, just as Comcast had done. For example, an ISP will imperceptibly delay some of the data "packets" of a long, high-definition movie to ensure that a short Skype call goes through without disruption. "Broadband networks handle some packets that must be delivered in tenths of a second to be useful as well as packets that aren't relevant for minutes or hours," says Bennett. "So it is absurd to treat all packets equally." But network neutrality, strictly understood, requires just that. If broadband operators are kept from performing such rational data management, the result will be a bias in favor of bandwidth monsters and against more-casual users.

Killing the Golden Goose

If you're a telecom lawyer, the creation of the Obamanet means that it's time to open the bubbly. Interest groups and lobbyists have "an open-ended invitation" to demand price controls and service mandates on ISPs – and even on "upstream" network operators like Amazon, Google, Twitter, and Facebook, business columnist Holman W. Jenkins Jr. writes. Title II applies to all "telecommunication services," a category that extends beyond ISPs to encompass any Internet services that send communications. Litigation will be never-ending, just as it has been for decades for wired telephone networks, which are subject to Title II regulations.

Potential violations of Title II by Internet-reliant firms positively leap to mind. Amazon has a special (which is to say, non-neutral) agreement with Sprint that lets Sprint users download e-books for their Amazon Kindles extra-speedily. As Crovitz points out, competing sellers of e-books can now claim that that agreement is unjust – and sue. Struggling BlackBerry has already invoked network-neutrality rules to petition the FCC to strong-arm Netflix and Apple into developing apps for BlackBerry devices, which no longer sell well. BlackBerry customers have been "discriminated against," claims CEO John Chen. Netflix will rue its extensive lobbying for network neutrality – driven by the hope of staving off higher broadband charges – if competitors use Title II to object to its special content-delivery arrangements that ensure that the firm's videos stream smoothly on various networks.

Even more troubling, perhaps, is that the Obamanet order includes a nebulous new "general conduct" rule that seemingly covers all activity on the Internet, giving government regulators the authority to stop any practices they deem harmful to "consumers, competition, or innovation." Asked what the rule meant in practice, FCC Chairman Wheeler candidly replied, "We don't really know. We don't know where things will go next." The FCC will act as a referee and "throw the flag," he promised – but in a game with shifting rules. The general-conduct rule disturbed even some supporters of network neutrality, like the Electronic Frontier Foundation. The nonprofit objected that it could "lead to years of expensive litigation to determine the meaning of 'harm.'" Lawyers and lobbyists will surely have lots to do.

Pervasive uncertainty will inevitably dampen competition, investment, and innovation. "If you were an entrepreneur trying to make a splash in a marketplace that's already competitive," Pai warned at a conference run by the nonprofit TechFreedom, "how are you going to differentiate yourself if you have to build into your equation whether or not regulatory permission is going to be forthcoming from the FCC? According to this, permissionless innovation is a thing of the past." The shift "represents an under-appreciated sea change in U.S. technology policy and one that is fundamentally inconsistent with the high-tech community's libertarian spirit," explains Yoo in *Fortune.* "Under this new approach, Silicon Valley is now under the protection of Washington and will need to come to policymakers for adjudication of

The Obamanet order offers no evidence of systematic harm to consumers to justify the FCC's sweeping takeover.

disputes." Getting an answer could take a while: "We decline to adopt fixed, short deadlines for resolving formal complaints," the FCC order says. Innovation will have an incentive to shift away from the Internet to less regulated sectors of the economy.

Broadband doesn't fall from heaven. Making it harder for ISPs to profit from the development and deployment of their costly networks will reduce their incentive to keep improving and growing those networks so that they can match the ever rising demand for bandwidth. Europe introduced a heavy-handed Title II–style Internet regulatory regime back in 2002, and it has clearly damaged the continent's broadband health. A recent study from the Internet Innovation Alliance found that European ISPs invested just $60 billion in 2011 and 2012 – about a third of what American ISPs did. A far smaller percentage of Europeans than Americans enjoyed high-speed Internet service, the report showed. "Without robust investment, competition cannot flourish," the study's authors concluded. The European Commission has recommended that its member states move away from the intrusive regulatory approach, even as the FCC has embraced it. Meanwhile, many smaller American broadband operators like Joink LLC – which serves more than 2,000 customers in Terre Haute, Ind. – have already announced that they're cutting back on expansion plans because of the Obamanet's compliance costs.

A Lesson From History

As *Washington Post* columnist Robert Samuelson argues, the history of America's railroads highlights the danger to innovation posed by the FCC's heavy hand. Congress created the Interstate Commerce Commission (ICC) in 1887 to ensure that the rates charged by railroads weren't discriminatory, just as the FCC intends to do with the Internet. As it turned out, Samuelson writes, "the railroads needed ICC approval for almost everything: rates, mergers, abandonments of little-used branch lines." Shippers ferociously resisted any changes that would add to their costs. Confronted with competition from trucks and barges, the railroads couldn't adapt, and they hemorrhaged money. The giant Penn Central railroad, which served the Northeast, went bust in 1970.

In 1980, President Jimmy Carter signed into law the Staggers Rail Act, deregulating the railroads. Writes Samuelson:

> *The ensuing deregulation succeeded brilliantly.… Costs and freight rates both declined. Railroads shed unprofitable lines and offered pricing packages that rewarded shippers for moving more freight in bulk. Mergers consolidated railroads into four major companies. Profits rose. The*

industry brags that it has spent $575 billion since 1980 to improve the rail network.

Utility regulation is no friend to innovation, as the railroad story shows – and as the stories of Ma Bell, power companies, and other public utilities show as well. Transforming the most explosive, fast-moving, and investment-attracting sector of the economy into something that resembles the local water company will have a similar effect.

Reclassifying the Internet as a utility may also mean new tolls for Internet users. Title II lets states and localities place fees on ISPs, just as they do on telecoms, and economists Robert Litan and Hal Singer believe those will get passed on to consumers. Internet bills, they think, "could soon have new random charges tacked on at the end, much like consumers see on their phone bills today." Estimates vary on exactly how much more we'll be paying, but Litan and Singer predict that the tab will easily add up to billions of dollars yearly.

* * *

The Obamanet will worsen a brand of arbitrary authority that has been metastasizing in Washington. As Randolph J. May – the president of the Free State Foundation think tank and a former associate general counsel of the FCC – elaborated in a column for the website the Hill, the FCC's ambiguous new rules will lead affected parties to seek exemptions or waivers from the FCC. That should worry anyone concerned about constitutional government. Drawing on the argument of Philip Hamburger's magisterial recent study *Is Administrative Law Unlawful?*, May recalls that one of the Founding Fathers' key objectives was "to control, if not eliminate, what in England was known as the 'dispensing' power" – a form of royal prerogative that let the king exempt himself, or those he favored, from complying with Parliament's laws. When administrative agencies like the FCC use waivers, May says, they're basically resurrecting the dispensing power. Here's Hamburger:

> *Like dispensations, waivers go far beyond the usual administrative usurpation of legislative or judicial power, for they do not involve law-making or adjudication, let alone executive force. On the contrary, they are a fourth power – one carefully not recognized by the Constitution.*

Administrative waivers, long part of the FCC's activities, are sometimes justified. But the expansion of the agency's authority is sure to bring a big increase in waiver seeking – and thus a big increase in the dispensing power of government regulators. In particular, maintains May, the new catchall "general conduct" rule all but guarantees that the agency will be "granting dispensations to some firms and not others based on the exercise of discretion untethered to any intelligible standard in any law enacted by Congress."

Needless to say, incumbent firms, with deep pockets and phalanxes of lobbyists, will win special treatment more often than aspiring newcomers will. What ISP startup could match an old Washington hand like AT&T on Title II terrain? No wonder the share prices of broadband titans rose as reclassification appeared imminent in early 2015 – and rose again in the weeks after the FCC officially announced its order. They may not like dealing with more government red tape, but the large, established cable and telecom firms know how to do it.

True, the FCC promises to "forbear" from applying hundreds of possible Title II restrictions on the Internet, including rate regulation, so as to "preserve incentives," as the FCC's Wheeler puts it. But nothing he says is binding or would prevent "future FCC chiefs and Washington's activist armies from charging through the door he just opened," says Jenkins. *Fauxbearance* would be a better term for the FCC's vow of restraint, contends the second dissenting FCC commissioner, Michael O'Rielly. The Obamanet is a recipe for influence peddling and political corruption.

* * *

An even more disturbing scenario would be an FCC move to curb political speech. "I could easily see this migrating over to the direction of content," warns Pai. "It is conceivable to me to see the government saying, 'We think the Drudge Report is having a disproportionate effect on our political discourse ... and we want to start tamping down on websites like that.'"

If you find such a scenario unlikely, recall that the FCC long enforced a Fairness Doctrine that required radio and broadcast television stations to cover "vitally important controversial issues of interest in the community served by the licensees" and provide "opportunity for the presentation of contrasting viewpoints on such issues." Until the Ronald Reagan–era FCC abandoned the doctrine in the 1980s, broadcasters had to look over their shoulders whenever they aired something potentially controversial. The FCC could fine violators, demand "free time" for views that the commission felt had been unfairly treated, and even remove operating licenses. The Fairness Doctrine got hijacked by politicians to attack their enemies, made broadcasters leery of political themes, and, in general, suppressed speech – as became clear once it was gone and issue-oriented talk radio, and later television's opinionated Fox News, boomed. The right was a big winner in this media liberation, finding a ready audience for arguments that traditional press outlets – dominated by liberal reporters, editors, and programmers – had often ignored.

One would like to believe that the Fairness Doctrine idea is dead and that the prospect of extending fairness regulations to the Internet's maelstrom of debate and expression would appear both unjust and unworkable on its face. In 2014, though, the FCC was ready to launch a Multi-Market Study of Critical Information Needs, with agency researchers interviewing employees of television and radio broadcasters to determine how stories got selected and whether the process was biased against or failed the needs of "underserved populations." Complaints

---

Would it be so awful if ISPs did charge customers more for lightning-fast lanes for heavy-bandwidth products – or for other innovations that treated data unequally?

---

by Republicans in Congress led the FCC to shelve the plan, at least for now. Leading Democrats, from Dianne Feinstein to Al Gore to John Kerry, have called for a restoration of the Fairness Doctrine in recent years. President Obama's former regulatory czar Cass Sunstein at one point mused about mandated "electronic sidewalks," which would offer alternative positions on partisan websites. And some of the same advocates who've battled for "equal treatment" of Internet data in broadband conduits also seem to want a political crackdown on web-expressed views that they don't like.

Consider Free Press, the group that spearheaded the pro-network-neutrality drive. Cofounder Robert McChesney, a University of Illinois communications professor who's "hesitant to say" that he's "not a Marxist," has been blunt about his group's long game. "We need to do whatever we can to limit capitalist propaganda, regulate it, minimize it, and perhaps even eliminate it," he said in a 2009 interview. "The fight against hyper-commercialism becomes especially pronounced in the era of digital communications." Not exactly a ringing endorsement of free speech or free markets.

Yet as *National Review*'s John Fund reports, Free Press – notwithstanding its "astonishingly radical goals" – has managed to insert itself directly into the FCC's operations and rulings. Obama's first FCC chairman, Julius Genachowski, hired Free Press's Jen Howard as his press secretary. Mark Lloyd, the co-author of a 2007 Free Press document on fixing the "structural imbalance" of political talk radio – that is, shutting up conservative hosts – was the commission's chief diversity officer from 2009 to 2012. Free Press's name shows up dozens of times in the Obamanet order. Pai's worries about the FCC's moving to regulate Internet content suddenly don't seem so far-fetched.

As the Obamanet dawned, Pai and a Federal Election Commission (FEC) counterpart, Lee Goodman, worried about a potential cross-agency attack on Internet liberties. In late 2014, they noted, the FEC had come perilously close – the commissioners were deadlocked three to three – to placing cumbersome disclosure requirements on political content that citizens and groups posted free on blogs, YouTube, social media, and other online platforms. The speech-squelching effect would have been immediate.

Surely the courts would shoot down such FCC or FEC restrictions on First Amendment grounds, right? Maybe, but the Supreme Court has never ruled the Fairness Doctrine unconstitutional; indeed, it justified it in a 1969 decision. The court also signed off in the not-so-distant past on a campaign-finance law that unquestionably hampered political speech, though it has retreated from that decision in more-recent cases. Given the leftward orientation of many courts and law schools, assuming that the judiciary will uphold robust political-speech rights is a risky bet.

In Praise of Regulatory Humility

The Obamanet needs to be dismantled before it can damage American prosperity and political liberty. How to do it?

A Republican president – or a less-liberal-than-Obama Democratic one – could appoint a freedom-minded FCC, which could restore the light-touch regulation that Title II reclassification replaced. Some Republican presidential hopefuls, including Ted Cruz and

Rand Paul, have denounced the FCC's action, probably making it an issue in the 2016 campaign. Congress could pass a new law reversing the FCC's power grab. Obama's intervention in the business of what's supposed to be an independent commission could lead the courts to overturn the FCC's move, just as they did for its earlier network-neutrality orders (though those previous defeats resulted from a cause that has evaporated: the commission's having exceeded the authority that it has now granted itself). Also, as neutrality critic Manne observes on Wired.com, "Supreme Court precedent ... makes clear that agencies may not adopt rules that 'run ... counter to the evidence before the agency,' or are simply implausible" – and the FCC seems guilty of both violations here. Lawsuits have already been filed.

A long-term step to protect the Internet would be for Congress to shut down the FCC entirely. As social theorist Peter Huber detailed in *Law and Disorder in Cyberspace*, his 1997 study of American telecommunications

Network neutrality is at odds with many of the now standard practices that have helped make today's Internet the market cornucopia that it is.

policy, the FCC was established during the late 1920s and early 1930s, an era that was gung-ho about command-and-control government and hostile to markets. "Around the globe, people in power persuaded themselves that the technical complexities of broadcasting, and the natural-monopoly economics of telephony, had to be managed through centralized control," writes Huber. "The night of totalitarian government, always said to be descending on America, came to earth only in Europe. But America was darkened by some of the same shadows." One was the

FCC – and though it has been friendlier to markets since the 1980s, its record over the decades exhibits many of the flaws typical of top-down planning. Swollen into a large bureaucracy – today it has 1,700 employees and a budget of more than $330 million – the commission has protected monopolies, mispriced various services, consistently impeded innovation, and curbed free speech.

Such actions have exacted an enormous toll on the U.S. economy. For example, if the commission had approved full competition for long-distance calls in 1968, when the idea first came before it, and not waited until 1980, consumers would have saved $16 billion – just one of many costly mistakes that Huber documents. A ponderous Washington agency propounding obdurate decrees, the FCC has never been able to keep pace with the rapidly mutating technologies and markets that it seeks to regulate. Had it treated the Internet as a public utility from the outset, the digital world would be much less vital today. The commission "should have been extinguished years ago," Huber believes.

Fiercer market competition would help protect the public from the prospective abuses that the Obamanet claims to save it from. At the moment, burdensome regulations imposed by local governments on ISPs – charging them unreasonable rates for access to government utility poles, requiring them to serve areas where there's no market demand, mandating that they offer free Internet to government offices, and so on – create needless barriers that are hard for new broadband competitors to hurdle. That hampers exciting projects like Google Fiber, which offers to bring great Internet speed to cities that are willing to loosen regulations. More localities should open their broadband markets and intensify ISP competition. (Google Fiber is another salutary development that the Obamanet could imperil, by the way. Perhaps that explains the search giant's seemingly shifting stance toward Internet regulation. Like Netflix, Google originally lobbied aggressively for network neutrality. By early 2015, however, executive chairman Eric Schmidt was telling White House officials that Title II was the wrong way to get it. With some academics and activists demanding "search-engine neutrality" these days, Google should be even more worried.)

Whether or not the FCC is abolished, there are agents that could better protect consumers from any anticompetitive actions by ISPs or other Internet companies: the more competition-minded Federal Trade Commission, the Department of Justice, and other litigators, all of them wielding antitrust and consumer-protection law. The advantage of this approach is that it is usually (though not invariably) far less intrusive than the FCC's sweeping-mandate-from-on-high modus operandi. When cases arrive at the FTC, the agency assesses them one at a time, explains Wright, "marshaling the available economic literature and empirical evidence" to see if actual harm has been done and, if it has, how best to address it – *in that case.* Yet another worrisome aspect of making the Internet a public utility is that it threatens to strip the FTC of its ability to protect consumers from deceptive advertising and other objectionable acts by ISPs.

Under the Obamanet, everything is prophylactically forbidden until it's allowed. The bias traditionally held by agencies charged with antitrust enforcement and consumer protection is the contrary: everything is permitted until it's not. That's the right way to approach the Internet, says FTC commissioner Maureen Ohlhausen, who also invokes a Hayekian philosophy of "regulatory humility." Regulators face a fundamental knowledge problem, she explained in a recent talk. Obtaining all the relevant information about an industry's present state and future trends is beyond the capacity of any one person or commission. After all, that information will be widely dispersed, and some of it will be tacit in the minds of the industry's actors or become obsolete by the time regulators get hold of it. That observa-

The Obamanet will worsen a brand of arbitrary authority that has been metastasizing in Washington.

tion is all the more applicable to the boundless, complex Internet economy. "The success of the Internet has in large part been driven by the freedom to experiment with different business models, the best of which have survived and thrived, even in the face of initial unfamiliarity and unease about the impact on consumers and competitors," Ohlhausen observed.

Liberating the Internet from the encroachments of Washington regulators would fire the further growth of one of the most remarkable inventions in human history – a "bountiful marketplace," in the words of economist Thomas W. Hazlett, that "has emerged unplanned, unregulated, from the visions of technologists, the risks of venture capitalists, and the innovations of entrepreneurs, large and small." Its wonders are a testament to human freedom, not to the presumed brilliance of government planners.

First American edition published in 2015 by Encounter Books, an activity of Encounter for Culture and Education, Inc., a nonprofit, tax exempt corporation.
Encounter Books website address: www.encounterbooks.com

Manufactured in the United States and printed on acid-free paper. The paper used in this publication meets the minimum requirements of ANSI/NISO Z39.48–1992 (R 1997) (*Permanence of Paper*).

FIRST AMERICAN EDITION

LIBRARY OF CONGRESS CATALOGING-IN-PUBLICATION DATA

Anderson, Brian C., 1961-
Against the Obamanet / Brian C. Anderson.
pages cm
ISBN 978-1-59403-849-5 (pbk. : alk. paper) —
ISBN 978-1-59403-850-1 (ebook)
1. Network neutrality--Government policy—United States.
I. Title.
HE7781.A76 2015
384.30973—dc23
2015020647

10 9 8 7 6 5 4 3 2 1

SERIES DESIGN BY CARL W. SCARBROUGH